THIS BELONGS TO

____

____

____

"Harmony Within:

101 Practical Ways to Embrace Tranquility and Reduce Stress in Your Daily Life"

In a bustling world filled with constant demands and rapid pace, there once lived a person seeking solace amidst the chaos. This individual, like many of us, longed for a sense of inner peace and tranquility. In the quest for a harmonious existence, they discovered the profound significance of cultivating a balanced and stress-free life. Embracing this journey, they explored various practical ways to find harmony within. From simple daily rituals to profound mindset shifts, each discovery became a stepping stone toward a more tranquil and fulfilling life. Now, armed with 101 practical strategies, this guide, "Harmony Within," invites you to embark on your own odyssey towards serenity. Let this be the beginning of your personal transformation, as you navigate the pathways to tranquility and discover the art of reducing stress in your daily life.

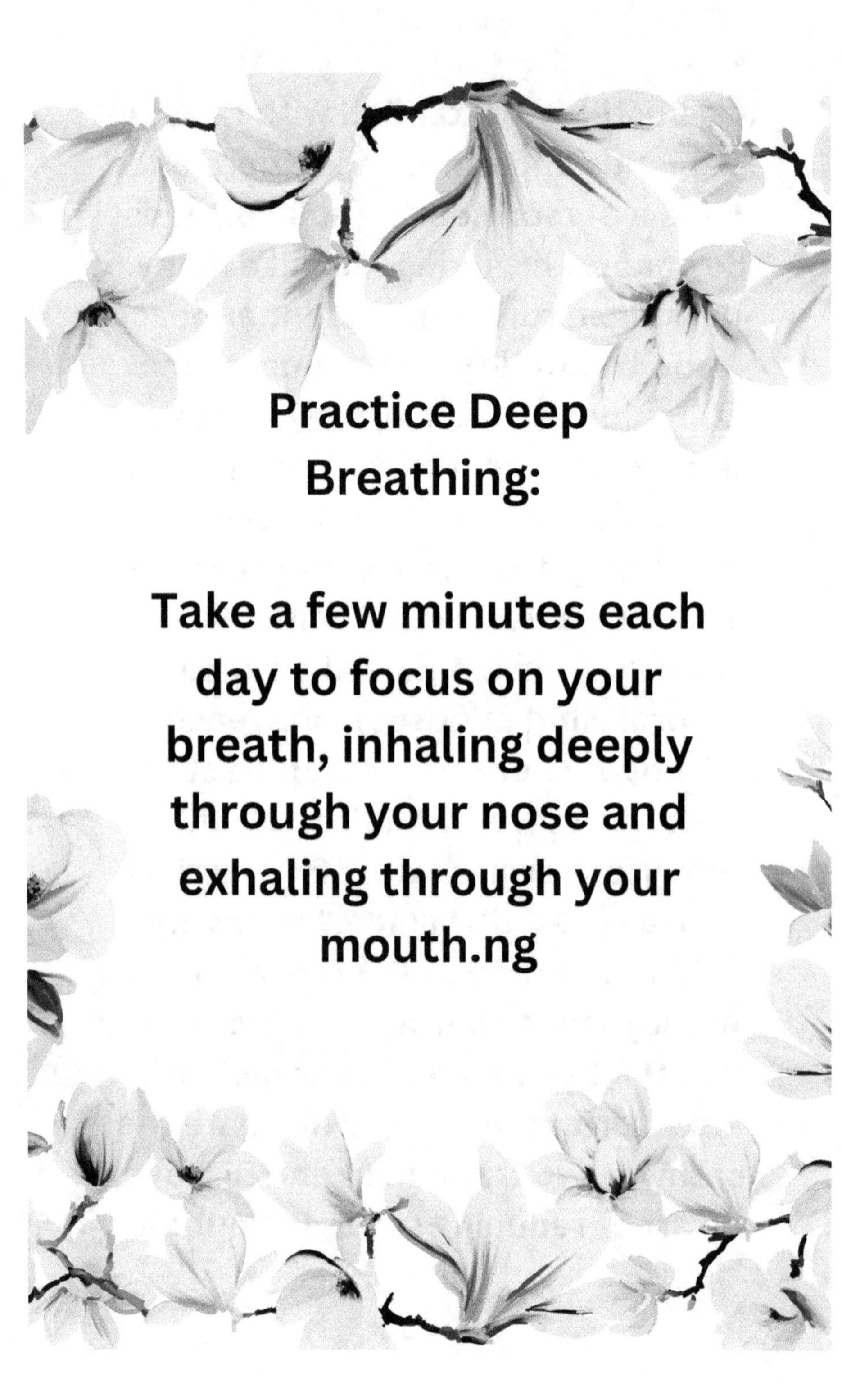

Practice Deep Breathing:

Take a few minutes each day to focus on your breath, inhaling deeply through your nose and exhaling through your mouth.ng

Set Realistic Goals:

Break down big tasks into smaller, more manageable goals to avoid feeling overwhelmed.

Prioritize Tasks:

Identify the most important tasks and tackle them first to create a sense of accomplishment.

Learn to Say No:

It's okay to decline additional responsibilities if you're already stretched.

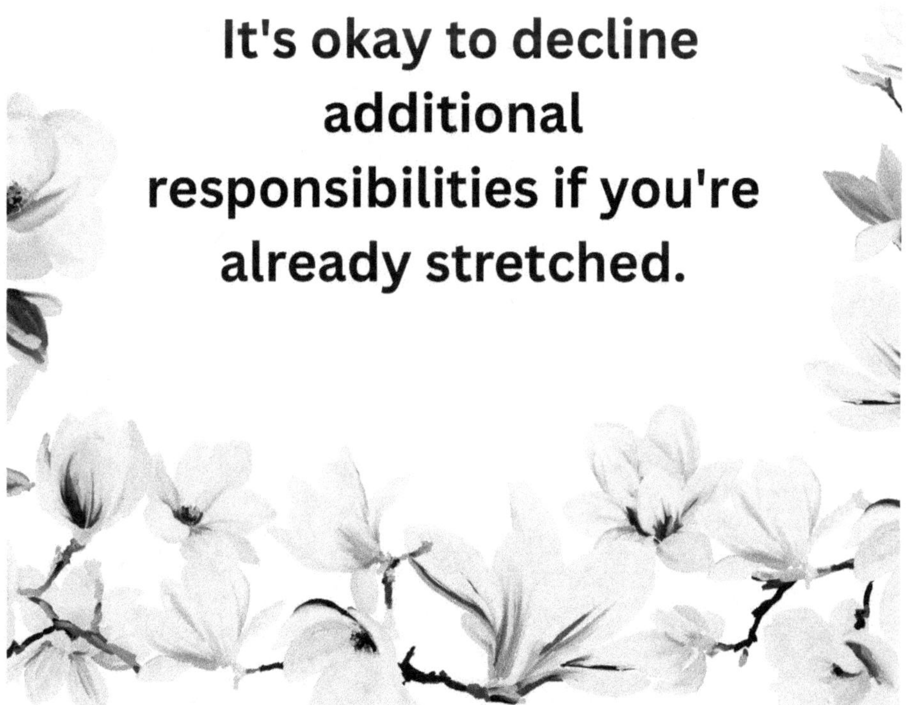

Establish Boundaries:

Set clear boundaries between work and personal life to prevent burnout.

Create a Relaxing Morning Routine:

Start your day with activities that bring you joy and set a positive tone for the day.

Limit Screen Time:

Take breaks from electronic devices to reduce mental fatigue and eye strain.

**Practice Mindfulness
Meditation:**

**Cultivate mindfulness
to stay present and
calm in the midst of
daily challenges.**

Get Adequate Sleep

Aim for 7-9 hours of sleep each night to support overall well-being.

Stay Hydrated:

Dehydration can contribute to stress, so ensure you're drinking enough water throughout the day.

Incorporate Regular Exercise:

Physical activity releases endorphins, which can help reduce stress and improve mood.

Cultivate a Positive Mindset:

Focus on the positive aspects of situations rather than dwelling on the negative.

Delegate Tasks:

Don't be afraid to ask for help or delegate tasks to lighten your workload.

Take Short Breaks:

Step away from your work periodically to refresh your mind.

Listen to Music:

Enjoy calming music to soothe your nerves and elevate your mood.

Practice Gratitude:

**Reflect on the things
you're grateful for to
shift your perspective.**

Journaling:

Write down your
thoughts and feelings as
a way to process and
release stress.

Laugh More:

Find humor in everyday situations and surround yourself with things that make you laugh.

Connect with Nature:

Spend time outdoors to enjoy the calming effects of nature.

Limit Caffeine Intake:

Excessive caffeine can contribute to feelings of anxiety, so moderate your intake.

Learn to Forgive:

Holding onto grudges can be a source of stress; practice forgiveness for your own peace of mind.

Read for Pleasure:

**Escape into a good
book to relax your mind.**

Attend a Yoga Class:

Yoga combines physical activity with mindfulness, promoting relaxation.

Declutter Your Space:

A tidy environment can contribute to a sense of order and calm.

Establish a Routine:

Predictability can
reduce stress, so create
a daily routine that
works for you.

Limit News Consumption:

Constant exposure to negative news can heighten stress levels; stay informed but set boundaries.

Learn Time Management:

Efficiently manage your time to avoid last-minute rushes and deadlines.

**Practice Progressive
Muscle Relaxation:**

**Tense and release
different muscle groups
to alleviate physical
tension.**

Volunteer:

Helping others can provide a sense of purpose and fulfillment.

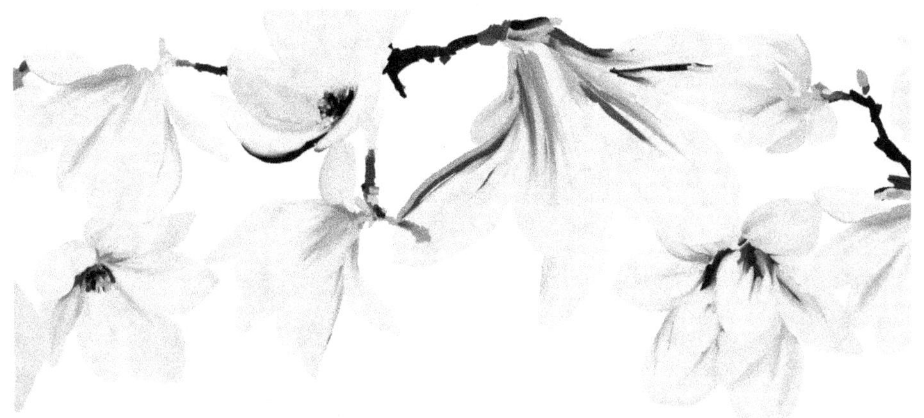

Use Aromatherapy:

Scents like lavender and chamomile can have calming effects.

Set Realistic
Expectations:

Be realistic about what
you can accomplish in a
given time frame.

Take Warm Baths:

Soaking in a warm bath can help relax your muscles and calm your mind.

Limit Social Media:

Reduce social media use, as it can contribute to feelings of inadequacy and stress.

Create a Budget:

Financial stress can be a major source of tension; create a budget to manage expenses.

**Practice the Pomodoro
Technique:**

**Break your work into
intervals, with short
breaks in between.**

Seek Social Support:

**Share your feelings
with friends or family
members for emotional
support.**

Learn to Let Go:

**Accept that some
things are beyond your
control and let go of
perfectionism.**

Visualize Success:

Picture positive outcomes to build confidence and reduce anxiety.

Experiment with Breathing Exercises:

Try different breathing techniques, such as box breathing or 4-7-8 breathing.

Learn to Distinguish Between Urgent and Important:

Focus on tasks that truly matter.

Explore Hobbies:

Engage in activities you love to recharge and relax.

Take a Digital Detox:

Disconnect from technology for a designated period to unwind.

Mindful Walking:

Pay attention to your surroundings and the sensation of walking to clear your mind.

Establish a Support System:

Surround yourself with people who uplift and support you.

Practice Self-Compassion:

Be kind to yourself, especially in times of difficulty.

Create a Vision Board:

Visualize your goals and aspirations to stay motivated.

Limit Perfectionism:

Accept that not everything needs to be perfect; aim for progress, not perfection.

Plan Mini Getaways:

Even short breaks can provide a refreshing change of scenery.

Plan Mini Getaways:

Even short breaks can provide a refreshing change of scenery.

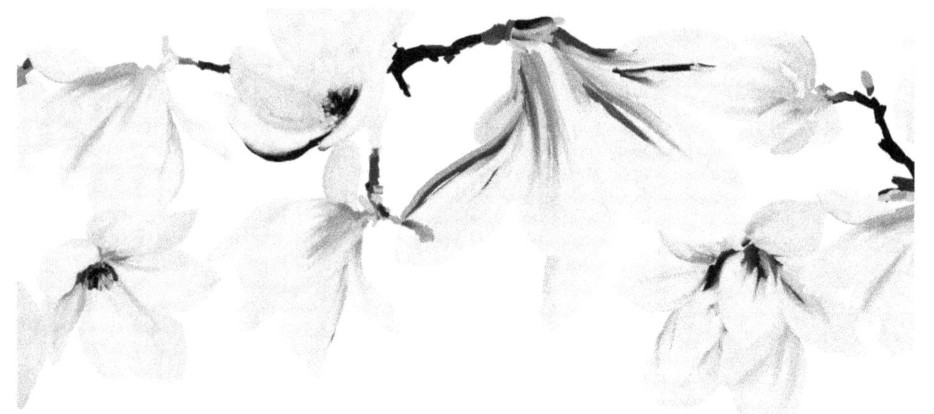

Express Yourself Creatively:

Engage in creative activities such as painting, writing, or crafting.

Learn to Delegate:

Trust others to share responsibilities and avoid taking on too much.

Dance It Out:

Move your body to music to release built-up tension.

stablish a "Worry Time":

Set aside a specific
time to address worries
rather than dwelling on
them throughout the
day.

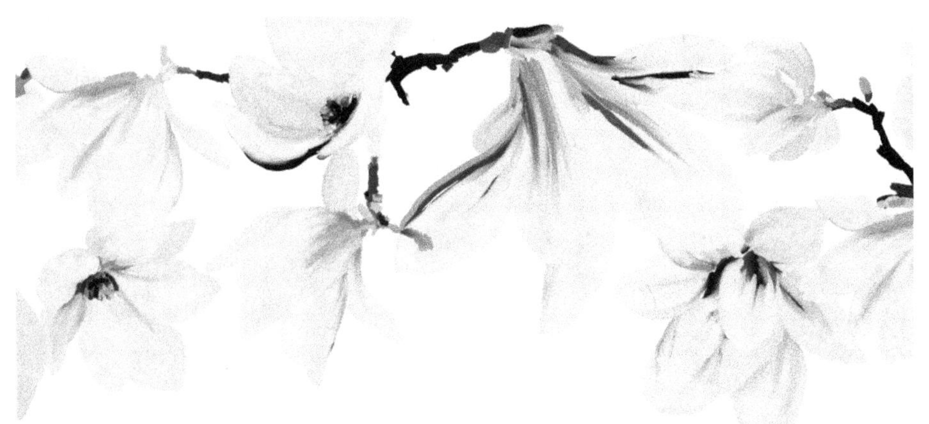

Try Cognitive Behavioral Therapy (CBT) Techniques:

Challenge negative thoughts and replace them with more positive ones.

Use Visualization:

Picture a calm and
peaceful place to
escape mentally.

Limit Perfectionism:

Accept that not everything needs to be perfect; aim for progress, not perfection.

Embrace the Power of "No":

Politely decline additional commitments that will add unnecessary stress.

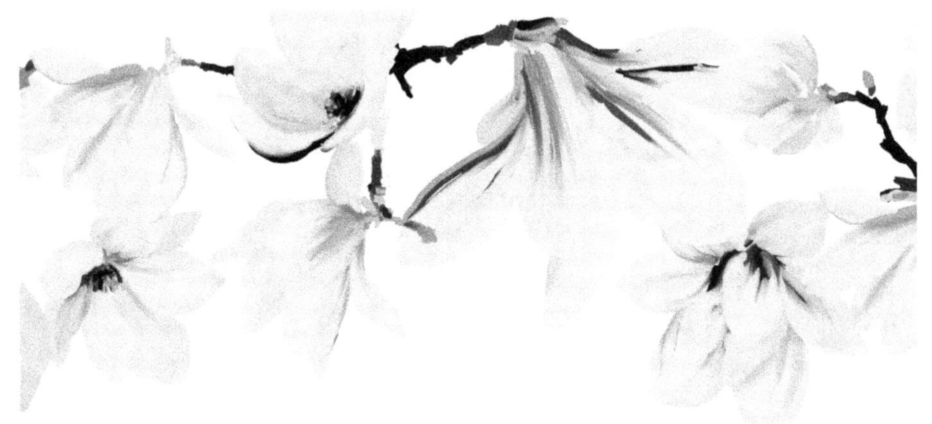

Create a To-Do List:

Organize tasks and
prioritize them to create
a sense of order.

Learn to Delegate:

Trust others to share responsibilities and avoid taking on too much.

Establish a "Worry Time":

Set aside a specific time to address worries rather than dwelling on them throughout the day.

Try Cognitive Behavioral Therapy (CBT) Techniques:

Challenge negative thoughts and replace them with more positive ones.

Use Visualization:

Picture a calm and
peaceful place to
escape mentally.

Limit Perfectionism:

Accept that not everything needs to be perfect; aim for progress, not perfection.

Create a To-Do List:

Organize tasks and
prioritize them to create
a sense of order.

Practice Acceptance:

Acknowledge that some things are beyond your control.

Write a Stress Journal:

Identify stressors and brainstorm solutions or coping mechanisms.

Practice the 5-4-3-2-1 Grounding Technique:

Name five things you can see, four things you can touch, three things you can hear, two things you can smell, and one thing you can taste.

Engage in Laughter Yoga:

Combine laughter with yogic breathing for a unique stress-relieving experience.

Cuddle with a Pet:

Spending time with animals can have a calming effect

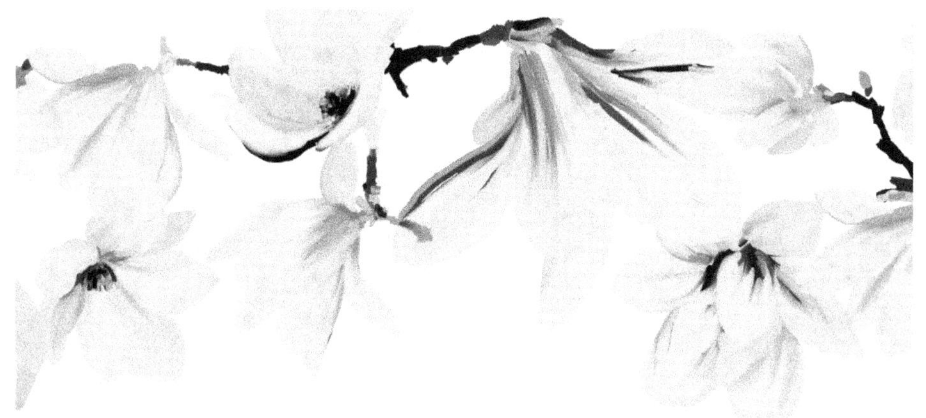

Try Biofeedback:

Use technology to
monitor and control
physiological functions,
helping you manage
stress

Establish a Bedtime Routine:

Create a calming pre-sleep routine to improve the quality of your sleep.

Express Your Feelings:

Share your emotions with a trusted friend or therapist.

Practice the "One-Minute Rule":

If a task takes less than a minute, do it immediately to avoid accumulating small stressors.

Create a Positive Affirmation:

4Develop a mantra that reinforces positivity and resilience.

Engage in Progressive Desensitization:

Gradually expose yourself to stressors to build resilience.

se Guided Imagery:

Listen to or create mental images that promote relaxation and well-being.

Establish a Self-Care Day:

Dedicate a day to self-care activities that rejuvenate your mind and body.

ake Advantage of Natural Light:

Spend time in natural sunlight to regulate your circadian rhythm.

Practice the 10-Second Rule:
Before reacting impulsively, take a brief pause to collect your thoughts.

Challenge Negative Thoughts:

Question and reframe negative thinking patterns.

Experiment with Herbal Teas:

Chamomile, valerian root, and lavender teas are known for their calming properties.

Create a "Joy" List:

Compile a list of
activities that bring you
joy and make time for
them regularly.

**Engage in Random Acts
of Kindness:**

**Doing something kind
for others can boost
your mood.**

Establish a Digital Sunset:

Limit exposure to screens in the hour before bedtime to improve sleep quality.

Learn to Let Go of Control:

Accept that you cannot control every aspect of your life.

Set Realistic Expectations for Others:

Recognize that people have limitations and may not always meet your expectations.

Practice Tai Chi or Qi Gong:

These gentle, flowing exercises promote relaxation and balance.

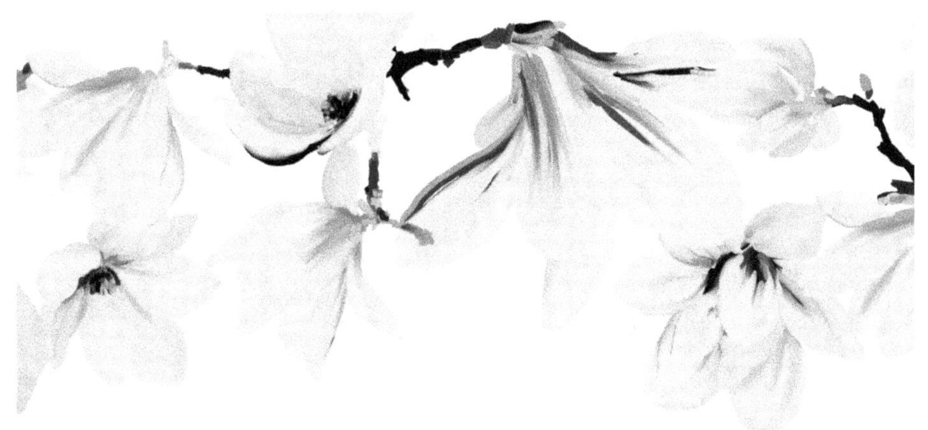

connect with Loved Ones:

Strengthening social connections can provide emotional support.

Utilize Stress Balls or Fidget Toys:

These can help release tension and redirect nervous energy.

Establish a "No-Complaint" Challenge:

Try to go a day without complaining, focusing on solutions instead.

Celebrate Small Wins:

Acknowledge and celebrate your achievements, no matter how small.

Try Acupressure:

Apply pressure to specific points on the body to relieve tension.

Use a White Noise Machine:

Create a soothing background noise to promote relaxation.

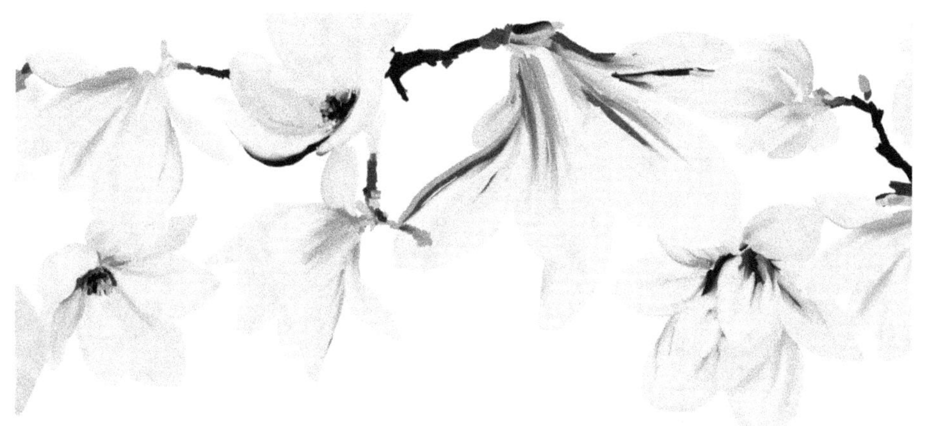

**Practice Emotional
Freedom Technique
(EFT):**

**Tap on specific meridian
points to alleviate
stress.**

**Express Yourself
Through Art:**

**Engage in painting,
drawing, or other
artistic activities as a
form of self-expression.**

Learn to Forgive Yourself:

Accept that everyone makes mistakes, and it's part of being human.

Practice Positive Self-Talk:

Replace self-critical thoughts with affirming and supportive statements.

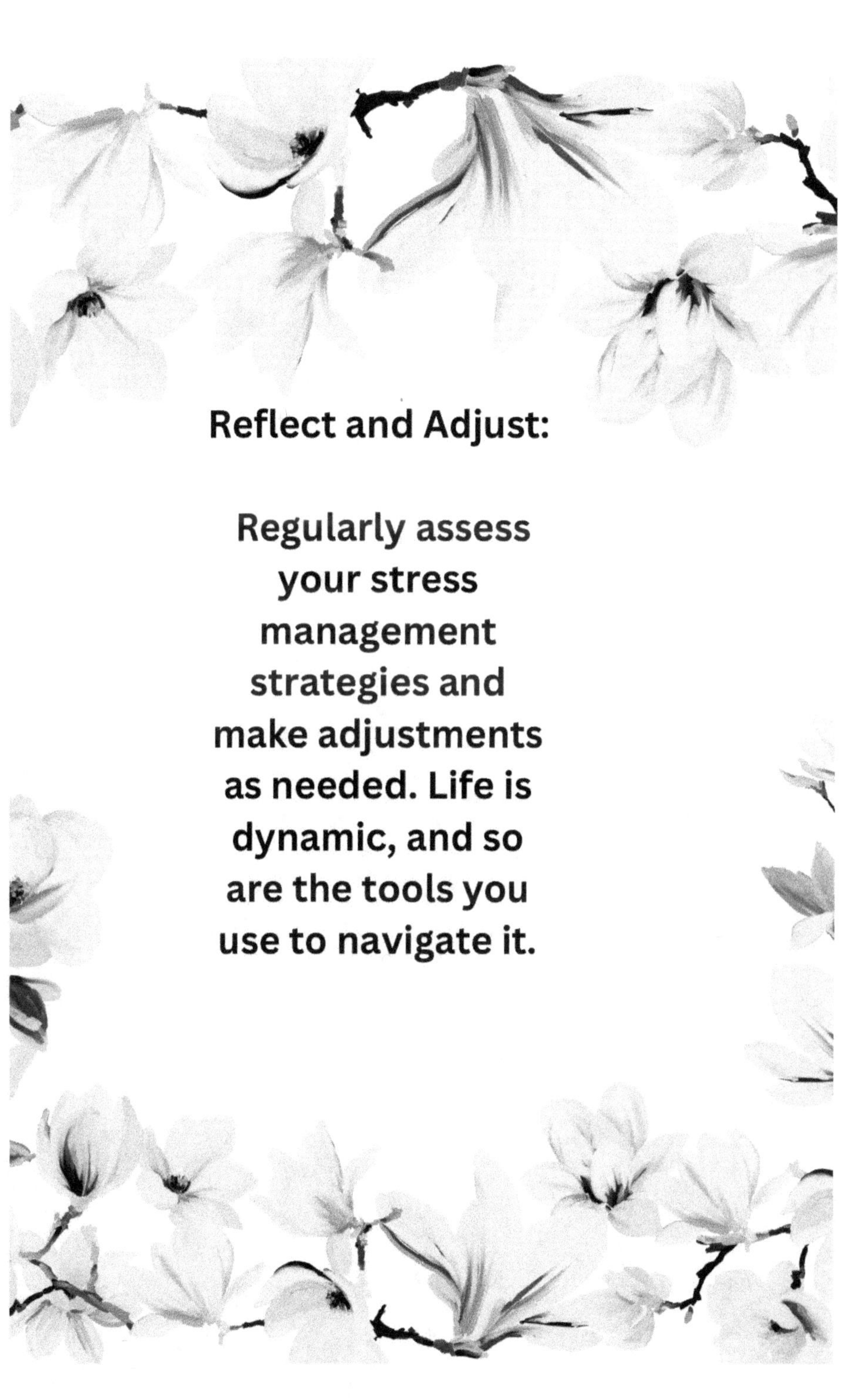

Reflect and Adjust:

Regularly assess your stress management strategies and make adjustments as needed. Life is dynamic, and so are the tools you use to navigate it.